A DEEPER WALK

BONNIE NILSSON

ISBN 979-8-88616-282-0 (paperback)
ISBN 979-8-88616-283-7 (digital)

Christian Faith Publishing
832 Park Avenue
Meadville, PA 16335
www.christianfaithpublishing.com

Printed in the United States of America

For Beni Johnson who went to be with the Lord
on July 13, 2022.

I have no idea where you are in your walk of faith. Perhaps you are looking for the path to faith as I was. This is my story. I write this as an imperfect guide based on my experiences. I did not need just a path to God. I needed a superhighway. My life that I knew fell apart in three days. I have always believed in God as a young child, and I was saved at seventeen years of age.

My life was going just as I had hoped and planned. I had beaten cancer once and had moved forward with a damaged self-image. I believed I was where I should be, and that was comforting. Then one beautiful fall week, my marriage fell apart on Monday, I lost my job on Tuesday, and I was told I had cancer on Thursday.

On Friday, I had a dream. I was in a carrot field, and a little rabbit stood next to me as I gazed ahead looking at a Willy Wonka kind of structure on the top of a hill. The building was puffing out orange smoke.

Immediately, the little rabbit said in a funny high-pitched voice like Bugs Bunny, "It's a juicer."

I knew the message was to drink carrot juice, and I did until my cheeks had a bronzed haze. I had avoided a repeat performance at the hands of medical experts. I was in a battle with my mind like no other.

This is where my path began, in a carrot field. Your path may have started somewhere else. Perhaps you did not even know you were in pursuit of a path, and *wham*, it hit you. A desire to know more consumed your thoughts. Thank God if that is your situation.

Experience is the best teacher. Why you ask? Experience is a highly personalized endeavor, which takes one's needs and wants into consideration, the motivation for why knowledge is being sought. Your birth order affects the interpretation of your experiences.

Knowing this, I choose not to focus on myself, but I chose to focus on the Godhead in whose image I am made in. May I suggest you do the same?

In Genesis 1:26,

And God said. Let Us make man in Our image after Our likeness.

I have read numerous books about Jesus Christ and Christian living. None of those books helped me get closer to God in the way I wanted. I believe we all know about faith, forgiveness, and that God can do all things; and we are to delight ourselves in the Lord. Knowing, believing, and experiencing are all very different. I like experiences. Being a nurse has shown me that experience can provide a wealth of knowledge.

Perhaps I wanted to really know that the Bible was true. More importantly, I wanted to know God the way the people in the Bible did.

CHAPTER 1

Why God?

In the beginning—the book of Genesis

MOSES HEARD FROM God as the Israelites were wandering in the desert. Moses was with God, and he received the Ten Commandments.

"I am the Lord thy God, thou shalt not have any gods before Me."

"Thou shalt not take the name of the Lord thy God in vain."

"Remember to keep holy the Sabbath day."

"Honor thy father and thy mother."

"Thou shalt not kill."

"Thou shalt not commit adultery." (includes all sexual sin)

"Thou shalt not steal."

"Thou shall not bear false witness against your neighbor." (or anyone)

"Thou shall not covet another's wife."

"Thou shall not covet your neighbor's goods."

Have you ever thought about how these commandments would apply to people wandering in the desert? People who had few belongings were all in the same plight as freed slaves, and God was keeping each one of them alive with shoes on their feet. As the Creator of man, God understood rules and boundaries provided safety. Can you be a slave one day and a self-directed human the next? The only example of which I am aware is Joseph in the Bible. Joseph spent two extra years in the dungeon because of unforgiveness toward his brothers. In Genesis 40:14, "But think of me when it shall be well with you, and show kindness, I pray you unto me, and make mention unto Pharaoh, and bring me out of this house."

God knows human nature. Human nature is what it is; some are just better than others. Christ's nature is the model that is the goal of every believer.

Of course, you say. I know that is the goal. What was it that Christ did of the many things He did while on earth that we should focus on? The greatest displayed action was His obedience to the will of God. That act of obedience made the cross possible.

The commandments were not written for Christ; they were written for God's people.

In Matthew 23:37–39,

> Thou shalt love the Lord thy God with all thy heart,
> and with all thy soul, and with all thy mind. This is the
> first and great commandment. And the second is like
> unto it, Thou shalt love thy neighbor as thyself.

I am imagining you might like to be closer to God if you only knew how. I write this book laying breadcrumbs for you to follow. This breadcrumb trail is between you and God. These are the steps I took to show God I cared about what He cared about. I cared more about pleasing God than man. My agenda could wait as I asked God what I could do for Him. Holy Spirit is whispering to you all the time if you have been born again with an indwelling of the Holy Spirit. The Spirit is our access to wisdom and knowledge.

I have read many great books on faith. I could not find a book that told me how to get closer to God.

How did I know God shows Himself at times with the occurrence of miracles regardless of who is in the surgery suite? That people would check out of the hospital avoiding the routine discharge process with a burst vessel only to check back in with a pulse. Once conscious, one patient said she saw streets of gold. Another said he was fishing with his brother who passed ten years earlier. Scans show that the vessels in question had been healed.

If you are born again, you have a direct connection to the divine by way of the cross and our Lord who gave His life so that we would have the key to His kingdom. As a parting gift, Jesus sent the Holy Spirit to help us today to comfort us, lead us, and guide us.

So this is my story. It is wild, scary, perplexing, sometimes unbelievable, and heartbreaking. I would not change any of it because I was never alone. I had a multitude of help and guidance.

I do believe if you take this message to heart, God will confirm it. You may begin to dream. Journaling can help you record the new experiences you will notice.

It may be advisable to be aware that as you head down this path, life may get a little messier than usual. That is the sign you are heading in the exact correct direction. The truth is, God never changes. We are His children, and I believe our obedience to the Holy Spirit affords favor.

You may feel like you are in test mode. I did. It seemed to me as I grew and gained greater discernment and had a better grasp of the written word of the Bible, more things requiring discernment were put in my path. I had to learn to trust what I was hearing. I always had a choice to make, and I soon learned to ask, What is the best choice, dear Lord?

The Holy Spirit is wisdom and understanding according to Isaiah 11:12. It is interesting to note after Isaiah was purged of sin, he offered himself to God's service.

When we look at the book of Genesis 1:26, we see that God said, "Let us make man in our image, after our likeness." God made the plant kingdom, the animal kingdom, and man. That was a big deal when God made the first man. The first man was Adam or Odom. There had never been a human anywhere before. God formed Adam, and He covered him with dirt. Then one day, God walked into the garden (the Garden of Eden). He got down brushing the dirt off of the form of Adam. God then laid on top of Adam's form and God put his fingers to Adam's fingers. His eyes to Adam's eyes. And with the same breath God used to create the world when He said, "Let there be light," He breathed life into Adam.

This is a beautiful tender story of God with the first member of His family. God made Adam as He desired a family. Angels are created beings, but they are not man. Man is made in the expressed image of God the Bible says.

Numbers 22:22 in the Old Testament is the first occurrence that Satan is mentioned in the Bible.

> How art thou fallen from heaven, O Lucifer, son of
> the morning! How art thou cut down to the ground,
> which didst weaken the nation. (Isaiah 14:12)

God knew about Satan. We might never know how heartbreaking it was for God to have Satan throw the first man, Adam, under the bus so to speak with the bite of an apple.

In Genesis 3:1,

> Now the serpent was more crafty than any of the wild animals
> the LORD God had made. He said to the woman, "Did God
> really say, 'You must not eat from any tree in the garden'?"

In Matthew 16:23,

> Jesus turned and said to Peter, "Get behind me, Satan!
> You are a stumbling block to me; you do not have in mind
> the concerns of God, but merely human concerns."

Get behind me is Jesus reminding Satan of the divine lineage. Satan would have loved to unseat Christ and budge man down the lineage chain. Taking out Adam's potential for greatness required Christ to restore humankind to God as He conquers hell and death.

> I am He that liveth, and was dead; and behold, I
> am alive for evermore, Amen, and have the keys
> of hell and of death. (Revelation 1:18)

My REM Sleep Disruption

I had sold my catering business and was doing some small business from home. I had all the tools I needed for my culinary endeavors. I must confess, I love to sleep. As a young person, I would sit on my bed and dream of the future. It was my safe place. Even as a hospitalized patient, I wrote my business plan while lying in bed.

So I was sleeping in my own bed, and the room was very dark. I was in REM sleep.

If you have children, you know when young, they will stand at the bedside and look at you, willing the slumbering mother to get up and make breakfast. I never really minded because it was a sweet way to start the day.

I had that feeling now, but who is looking at me? As I partly opened my eyes, I saw a four-foot cookie cutter shape of an angel in blazing white light, and the room was not lit. I was perplexed and confused. I didn't have a great deal of biblical understanding, and I was thinking of my paternal grandmother who was a very sweet and godly woman. She came to America as a nanny.

The gravelly voice rushed in and spoke in a direct manner of speech: "Slit your wrists and kill yourself. You will die." Blah, blah, blah. "He doesn't love you." Blah, blah, blah.

I was mad. *You're coming out of left field*, I thought. I just fought with almost everything I had to live. I rolled out of bed and felt a forty-pound rock on my back. I walked bent over to the living room and called out: "Jesus, help me." The weight instantly disappeared.

> Submit yourselves, then, to God. Resist the devil,
> and he will flee from you (James 4:7)

I was shaken and disoriented as I sat at the kitchen table until the sun rose. I had three good friends and asked them to call their perspective ministers if they would be so kind to find time to see me as soon as able.

The first minister arrived about 9:00 a.m. He was very concerned and asked me a lot of questions. Was I saved? Born again? Yes,

I was. After listening to my tale of horror, he said I should consult a doctor. It may be PTSD. I thanked him for his time and took his card so that I could send a contribution to his church.

The second minster arrived shortly after. He had nice eyes and said he was sorry that whatever it was that got me twisted up could be corrected. That was good news. After reading some scriptures, he asked if I considered I might be having a nervous breakdown. I was momentarily struck dumb. I thanked him and took his card so that I could send a contribution to his church.

At 1:00 p.m., the Baptist minister knocked on the door. He was lively. His demeanor intrigued me and frightened me at the same time. He asked a few questions. I did not know what he was thinking, and I prayed he did not judge me. He wasn't calling the ambulance, was he? Oh, how he laughed.

"Sweetheart, don't ask me why God allowed Satan to bother you. But for some reason, God wants you to know Satan is real."

I wanted to kiss the man; he hit the bull's-eye.

> And no wonder Satan himself is transformed into
> an angel of light. (2 Corinthians 11:14)

I was disoriented for a few days. This is not the kind of thing you tell anyone. Who would believe you? I hadn't met those folks yet. I learned years later that God did indeed allow that experience for my understanding.

Three weeks later, I got a call from the nursing department at a local college. Did I want to be in the nursing program starting the following week? They were offering a scholarship that had come in from an unusual source and were given my number. I was conflicted. I still didn't know who I was. It was a bit like living in a dream. Cancer survivors and others who had survived really bad events will often say their life took on a different feeling after survival. The things you once had a passion for meant nothing, and you could spend countless hours daydreaming. I really did not feel like the perfect nursing candidate, but a scholarship is a scholarship.

CHAPTER 2

God's Promise

God made promises to Noah (Genesis 9:9–11)

And behold I establish My Covenant with you, and with you
your seed after you And with every living creature that is with
you of the fowl and the cattle and with every beast of the earth
with you from all that go out of the Ark to every beast of the
earth And I will establish My Covenant with you, neither
shall all flesh be cut off anymore by the waters of a flood
neither shall there be any more a flood to destroy the Earth

God made promises to Abraham (Genesis 12:2–3)

The Lord said unto Abraham Get thee out of your country and
from your kindred and from your father's house, unto a land I
will show you. And I will make of you a great nation and I will
bless you and make your name great. And you shall be a blessing

God made promises to Abraham and Sarai (Genesis 17:15–16)

And God said unto Abraham, As for Sarai your wife, you shall
not call her Sarai but Sarah will her name be. And I will bless

her, and give you a son also for her: Yes, I will bless her and she shall be a mother of nations; kings of people shall be of her.

God made promises to Jacob (Genesis 35:10–11)

And God said unto him, your name is Jacob; your name shall not be called Jacob anymore, but Israel shall be your name; and He called his name Israel. And God said unto him, I am God Almighty; be faithful and multiply; a nation and a company of nations shall be of you, and kings shall come out of your loins.

USE AN ONLINE scripture site or your own Bible to fill in the promises God made to Moses and David.

God made promises to Moses (Exodus 5:22–6:12)

____

____

God made promises to David (2 Samuel 7:8–11)

____

____

God's promises to man (there are hundreds of examples in the Bible)

In Psalm 1:3,

That person is like a tree planted by streams of
water, which yields its fruit in season and whose leaf
does not wither—whatever they do prospers.

In Psalm 27:10,

When my father and my mother forsake me,
then the LORD will take me up.

In Psalm 31:24,

> Be of good courage, and He shall strengthen your
> heart, all you who hope in the Lord.

In Ephesians 2:8–9,

> For by grace you are saved through faith and that not of
> yourselves; it is a gift of God least any man boast.

> The Word became flesh and made his dwelling among us. We
> have seen his glory, the glory of the one and only Son, who came
> from the Father, full of grace and truth. (John 1:14 NIV)

> Then he said, When I was with you before, I told you that
> everything written about me in the law of Moses and the
> prophets and in the Psalms must be fulfilled. Then he opened
> their minds to understand scripture. (Luke 24:44–45)

The wisdom of God is ancient

> But to those called by God to salvation, both Jews
> and Greeks, Christ is the power of God and the
> wisdom of God. (1 Corinthians 1:24)

The Holy Spirt is the vehicle Jesus used to impart knowledge to the children of God. That's us.

> The Spirit of the LORD will rest on him—the Spirit of wisdom
> and of understanding, the Spirit of counsel and of might, the
> Spirit of the knowledge and fear of the LORD. (Isaiah 11:2)

The Holy Spirit is wisdom, understanding, counsel, might, knowledge, and fear of the Lord.

Luke was the first Book of the Bible that I understood well. I marvel that Paul who was never in the presence of Jesus had received by way of the Spirit a profound understanding of the scriptures. He had a vision of Christ sitting at the right hand of God the Father, and he became a prominent voice for the new church movement following the death of Christ. Paul began writing in AD 50 as he traveled his world, planting churches. He wrote thirteen books of the Bible. His scribe would write the words which Paul spoke to the churches. Paul was a lofty speaker who was a martyr for Christ around AD 67. Paul wrote these Gospels:

- Romans
- 1 and 2 Corinthians
- Galatians
- Ephesians
- Colossians
- 1 and 2 Timothy
- Titus
- Philemon

It is important to note that Luke has been credited by the biblical scholars to have the most accuracy in the written text. I do not find that a surprise as Luke was a trained physician who was called the beloved physician.

In Luke 1:1–4,

Forasmuch as many have taken in hand to set forth in order a
declaration of these things which are most surely believed among us
Even as they delivered them unto us which from the
beginning were eyewitnesses, and ministers of the Word
It seemed very good to me also, having had perfect
understanding of all the things from the very first to
write unto you in order most excellent Theophilus
That you might know the certainty of those
things wherein you have been instructed.

Theophilus is mentioned by Luke speaking as to someone who was a friend of God, and it is believed addressing him is the most excellent suggests Theophilus's stature in the Roman Empire or a man of means in Antioch.

In comparison, Paul is recorded as having this conversation. Paul in the book of Acts 26:25,

"I am not insane, most excellent Festus," Paul replied. "What I am saying is true and reasonable."

This verse leads us to consider that Paul has just been labeled as insane by a Roman official.

It would make sense that Luke was in the company of learned and wealthy men while Paul had come from the Roman soldiers, and those were his contemporaries from his life before the Spirit of God struck him off that horse and closed his sight with a vision of Christ at the right hand of God Almighty.

I believe we rarely consider the geopolitical climate of Jesus's time. We think today is bad with censorship and unfriendly governmental actions. The scripture doesn't give many clues, but one need only imagine the Roman Empire and the Sanhedrin both took brutal actions toward the followers of Christ. Those with power will never give it up, and we need to know God is greater. It is imperative that Christians worldwide learn to hear the Spirit of God as He utters instructions for our benefit in these times. The best way to hear the spirit is to be obedient to God in big things and small. We have this assurance:

In the last days, God says, I will pour out my Spirit on all people. Your sons and daughters will prophesy, your young men will see visions, your old men will dream dreams. (Acts 2:17)

John the Evangelist was the longest living disciple of the group of twelve, and James, his younger brother, was the first martyred for Christ AD 62 by stoning. Their mother named Zebedee, was the sister of Mary, the woman who was Jesus's mother.

Jesus called His cousins John and James the Sons of Thunder for their zeal. John was one of John the Baptist's disciples. It is believed that Apostle John wrote the book of Revelations AD 96. He wrote the book while at Patmos. John was the longest-living disciple. His death in AD 97 closed out a generation.

I enjoy thinking about the first church. It's so easy for us to Monday morning quarterback; however, the truth is they faced many struggles with the Elite Jewish leaders, the Sanhedrin an elite Greek ruling council, the Roman Empire, and others that were a clear and present danger to the workings of the first church.

If you have read the Bible from front to back, you will have spent a dedicated amount of time. It is advisable to do just that. I found reading the New Testament has many references to Old Testament Scripture. Eventually, God uses all of the Bible as He communicates by way of the Spirit to help you as you grow in biblical knowledge. Some biblical teachings will be of greater interest to you than others. I do believe the Bible is the greatest book ever written. And it is a huge history book filled with stories that once understood will help you to have a better understanding of the ways of God.

In 1 Corinthians 2:10,

But God hath revealed them unto us by way of the His Spirit;
For the Spirit searches all things. Yea the deep things of God.

In John 16:7,

Nevertheless I tell you the truth; It is expedient for you that
I go away; for if I go not away; the Comforter will not come
unto you; but If I depart, I will send him unto you.

It was my experience that churches that emphasize the office of the Godhead are rare in the part of America where I live. The foretelling of Christ and the great works that Jesus had accomplished is well preached. The equally important role of the Spirit to help keep the believer with access to the divine is not.

The Godhead is a triune. The Lord your God in the commandments and in the Book of Genesis is the creative power of the Godhead. We must welcome the Holy Spirit into our homes, our friendships, our marriages, our places of work, and certainly our places of worship. I sensed a voice or maybe more like a thought, and at first, I thought it was me, my own thought. Then I began paying more attention and thanking the Spirit for the information I believed I was being given.

Walmart's Garden Center

I had been a nurse for three years. I was working in a surgical step-down role. I worked shifts. There was an LPN who worked with me every three weeks or so, sometimes every other month. Something would always go down when we worked together. Always. Codes. Death is sometimes followed by life. I think we must have been doing some good in those tragic times. Maybe that is why we had those remarkable experiences. When we walked into the morning report together, the entire room would go, "Oh, no," referring to our reputation.

To get them going, I would say, "Well, buckle up and hang on." The room would always go wild.

Artist Jose Hernandez has a YouTube of his NDE experience. Any of you reading this who have routinely resuscitated people will find his testimony impactful. There is a real message for health care workers if you listen closely to his tale.

So I have a glorious day off, and it isn't raining. My new neighbor is not someone with whom I have a real relationship. She was also a nurse, and yet we struck no common chord. She would yell at the boys as they drove down the hill on our lot line and turn around and barrel up the hill and into the woods. She threatened civic action, and I said, "Use your common sense and stay safe in those woods," as the boys screamed in delight as they flew by laughing.

As I walked in through the Garden Department at my favorite Walmart, my cart bumped over the sidewalk, and there was a peck basket of a variety of pink pansies on the concrete to my right. Pink is my favorite color. Nancy would like those. There it was again, that voice that is a thought that is pushing or prodding me into action. I said something like, "Are you kidding me?" I knew it wasn't a joke. I was being offered an opportunity to make a bad situation better. She was my neighbor after all. I put the peck basket in my cart and headed to the grocery section of the store.

I returned home after shopping and took a note card and wrote,
Dear Nancy, I found these adorable flowers, and I hope you
have room in your garden for them. Enjoy the day today!
I left the note and the peck basket on her front door step.

I went to a late lunch with friends and returned to a note on my door. It was from Nancy. She had room in her garden. She loves pink. Perfect.

I hadn't seen Nancy for a few weeks, and I asked the neighbor across the street, "Have you seen her lately?"

"She moved to the Midwest, and she left last week," he said.

I marveled at my ability to hear and more importantly obey during a frenzied shopping run. I thanked the Holy Spirit for the suggestion.

Should she and I ever meet in an airport or on a beach, we can embrace one another and say, "Wow, you look fabulous. How've you been?"

In Matthew 22:37–39,

Thou shalt love the Lord thy God with all thy heart,
and with all thy soul, and with all thy mind. This is the
first and great commandment. And the second is like
unto it, Thou shalt love thy neighbor as thyself.

CHAPTER 3

The Word in Action

For He is our peace, who hath made both one, and hath broken down the middle wall of partition between us. (Ephesians 2:14)

SEVERAL CALAMITIES HAD been averted, and problems erased over the years because I knew that I knew. My friends, even my Christian friends, asked, "How did you know?" The believers who followed Christ had been instructed after His death and resurrection to go to the upper room. They were obedient, and they did as they were told. Once in the upper room, Acts 2:3 says:

> They saw what seemed to be tongues of fire that
> separated and came to rest on each of them.

Oh, yes. The Holy Spirit.

I have been in a group when a prophetically illogical instruction was uttered by another. I have to laugh because a lot of my instructions requiring obedience can be rather illogical at times. The group started chatting up, "Why should we do that? What sense does that Make?" And on and on.

There is no perfect Christian among us, and this Christian walk is not a competition. This is your walk with your Creator. Can you imagine when you realize the Spirit has been whispering, getting into

15

your thoughts how amazing your life with Christ can be? Can you imagine how you can be used for the greater things of God when you can understand the role He has chosen you for?

In the beginning, I prayed and asked God and the Spirit to tell me an instruction three times. I felt the enemy was interfering in a way I did not understand. I was still unsure, but my faith in God was growing.

The first word came over the TV on the weather channel. *Why am I getting Illinois weather? I missed that clue.* I ran out to do a few errands, and I was at the grocery store buying creamer for coffee. There was a man sitting at a table, reading the sports page with a feature about the Bruins on the back page. I missed that clue also. I stopped to get gas, and there were two men, one in front of my car and the other on my side.

"Hey," one guy said, "How've you been?"

"Lots of work been living in Chicago two weeks at a time," the other man said.

I get in my car having pumped my gas and looked to the car roof. *Are you kidding me? Chicago?* I asked.

I had already declined that opportunity. I had made up my mind, and I wasn't going to Chicago.

It would take all the money I had if I was to do what God was implying I should do. I didn't say I would go, and I suppose God could see I also gave up the fight. I would not exactly call it obedience on my part. I remember feeling it was some kind of test.

I am telling you this because we are more alike than we are different. We are of the same human race.

So I packed my bags, and I went to Chicago. Many times, you will not know what your presence in a certain setting is intended to do. I have never been called anywhere that it wasn't immediately apparent to me what my role would be once I arrived. This instance involved my current understanding of the covenant of marriage, and at a later time, my understanding was greatly enhanced. That was my first assignment, and there have been hundreds that have followed.

I had been at a ministry event, and I sat drinking coffee when a man asked if he could join me. He must have sensed my mild alarm.

I am an introvert by nature. I was far away from home. I didn't come to this event to make friends. He said to me, "I know you have been waiting, and it won't be much longer."

Was he serious?

As we sipped coffee, he said he was a recovered alcoholic. I congratulated him. He then told me God had been using him to work on other alcoholics. He said the Spirit would tell him an address, and he'd say, "Oh, not there. I can't go there."

He said one night it was cold and raining, and he went to the place that was mentioned. One person was in the bar.

As this man who was a recovered alcoholic stood inside the doorway, the bartender said, "Get out."

"I just want a coke, not going to say a word."

"No, out. Don't want any," was the reply.

The man was grieved when I met him, and he said the bartender had passed later that night a few nights prior. I could feel this man's angst.

I heard like someone was calling my name, "Tell him I sent the very best I had."

"Yes, I know it must hurt, but God is very clear when He says He sent His very best. He sent you," I said.

Prayer

Prayer is a well-established tradition in the Bible.

1.   Intercessory prayer

When you pray this type of prayer, you are interceding. Often this is not a prayer about you or your circumstance but a prayer for another. Regardless of the desired outcome of prayer, pray with faith and thanksgiving.

In Timothy 2:1,

> Therefore I exhort first of all that supplication prayer,
> intercessory, a thanks is made for all men.

2.　Prayer of confession

In James 5:16,

Confess your trespasses to one another, that you may be healed.
The effective fervent prayer of a righteous man avals much.

3.　Prayer of thanksgiving

This can be a daily prayer that I call soup to nuts.
Jesus, you are amazing, and, Holy Spirit, you are a wonderful counselor. Father God, you are absolutely good. I am adoring you today with a glad and thankful heart. Blessed be the name of the Lord God.

4.　Pray without ceasing

In 1 Thessalonians 5:16–18,

Rejoice always and pray without ceasing in all circumstances
　　　　for this is the will of God, in Christ for you.

When you pray, open your palms toward heaven to receive from God.
Let's pray:

> *Dear Heavenly Father,*
> 　*I thank you for this day. I believe in the truth of God's word and the power of His might to bring salvation. I repent from my sins this day and ask you, dear Jesus, not leave me as you find me but bring me the helper who is the Holy Spirit to open my eyes, bringing wisdom, understanding, knowledge, and healing so that I may impact your kingdom as I dedicate my life to you in truth.*
> 　*Amen (amen means truth)*

> Taste and see that the LORD is good: blessed is the
> man that trusteth in him. (Psalm 34:8)

Taste and see that the Lord is good. His goodness endures forever

I was saved when I was seventeen years old in a Pizza shop during basketball season. A musical band came from California to the east coast, and they found me. (Actually, they found us. Seven of us gave our lives to Christ that afternoon.) It was a demonstrative move of the Spirit, and the local church didn't really know what to do with the seven of us.

I would go to college and graduate with high honors from criminal justice. I fell in love, sight unseen. Trouble started happening, but I chose not to see it. I conceived a child. I loved being pregnant. More trouble that would put me in a hospital bed for six and one-half months. We would call it a demonic attack in hindsight. I did not go into the line of work for which I was trained. I was certain detective work suited me well. I got high marks on the rifle range. I owned no gun and never have.

My husband was bringing in food from home for me to eat while I was in the hospital. The smell of the food caused people to inquire from my hallway door. Did you get that at the café? These were pharmacy reps I later found out. I shared my creations with those men on paper towels, food that had been frozen for six months or more. They were my first customers when I opened my catering business two years after leaving the hospital. I was trying to find out who I was. I somehow lost the blueprint to my own life. Priorities change once you have survived a near wipeout, a wipeout not related to extreme sports or careless behavior.

This was more like part of your life was being stolen.

The thief comes only to steal and kill and destroy. (John 10:10)

The Roman Empire and the Sanhedrin of the elite ruling class of priests and lay people. Saul of Tarsus was one such man. In a blink of an eye, he becomes the most prolific speaker for the works of Christ and the power of the cross to save. Paul pens thirteen of the gospels as he traveled his world winning souls and preaching the truth of the Gospel of the ministry of Jesus.

In Acts 7:54–60,

> Now when they heard this, they were cut to the quick, and
> they began gnashing their teeth at him. But being full of
> the Holy Spirit, he gazed intently into heaven and saw the
> glory of God, and Jesus standing at the right hand of God;
> and he said, "Behold, I see the heavens opened up and
> the Son of Man standing at the right hand of God."
> But they cried out with a loud voice, and covered their ears
> and rushed at him with one impulse. When they had driven
> him out of the city, they began stoning him; and the witnesses
> laid aside their robes at the feet of a young man named Saul.
> They went on stoning Stephen as he called on the Lord and
> said, "Lord Jesus, receive my spirit!" Then falling on his
> knees, he cried out with a loud voice, "Lord, do not hold
> this sin against them!" Having said this, he fell asleep.

A cold autumn night

I will never forget my very first word when the pastor called me out of the crowd. I had been a strong Christian for several years, and a friend said there is a preacher from Vietnam, and he has a strong prophetic voice.

Okay.

We get to the country church a ways away. The house was packed. It was November. There were a lot of people in front, and you could hear the voice of the prophet above the quiet hum. God was there. You could feel it. I was praying, and I felt a gaze on me. I knew no one here other than my friend who drove me.

The prophet was standing upfront, and he was pointing at me in the back row. "I have a word for you. Come here if you would like to receive it," he said.

I fought my way to the front, squeezing between people and trying not to get lost in the crowd. I have never been someone who could see over the crowd. I prayed for that for two years. I witnessed a blue eyeball manifest into a socket and cauliflower ear turn normal. I knew God could stretch my femur bone. It would be easier than stretching the fibula, which goes to the ankle. I'll tell you the story that goes with that nonevent another time.

I am up at the front, and it has the heavy presence of God. I had trouble standing.

The prophet began speaking, "God has a word, and it is to stand. The gates of hell are open on you, and it is going to get worse before it gets better. But in the end, you will know God's purpose and plan, and you will be given the key to bind."

Everyone was silent. I was stunned and thankful, so very thankful that God DID know how beaten up I was. That word caused me to have hope, and that is what a prophetic word is supposed to do.

CHAPTER 4

Holy Spirit

The Father God, His Son Jesus, and the Holy Spirit:
The book of Genesis chapter 1

WRITTEN 4004 YEARS before Christ, the first chapter begins, "In the beginning God created heaven and earth. And the Earth was without form, and void; and darkness was upon the face of the deep and the Spirt of God [the Holy Spirit] moved upon the face of the waters."

Here is the first mention of the Spirit of God in the bible. Then again in Genesis 1:26 And God said. Let Us make man in Our image after Our likeness.

The Godhead is a triune; God the Father Almighty. God the creator also was with us in our mother's wombs.

Ephesians 1:17 That the God of our Lord Jesus Christ, the Father of glory, may give unto you the Spirit of wisdom and revelation in the knowledge of him.

Water Baptism at 11:00 a.m. and Work at 3:00 p.m.

I wanted to be baptized in water. I understood the significance of it. It is a summer day obviously, and I had to be at work at three that day. It was eleven in the morning. I was tenth in line as people were being dunked into the water for water emersion by the pastor. It was a fun scene actually.

I was next as I waded into the lake's water and became highly alert as the cold water engulfed me, and I went under. As I came up from the water directly ahead, I saw a huge nonsymmetrical red beating heart against the blue sky and noted slightly to my left the crowd of witnesses jammed tight into the choir loft hanging in the air.

He will baptize you with the Holy Spirit
and with fire. (Matthew 3:11)

In Psalm 139:13–14,

For you created my inmost being; you knit me together in
my mother's womb. I praise you because I am fearfully and
wonderfully made; your works are wonderful, I know that full
well. Your eyes saw my unformed body. All the days ordained for
me were written in your book before one of them came to be.

In Jeremiah 1:5,

Before I formed you in the womb I knew you, before you were
born I set you apart; I appointed you as a prophet to the nations.

The Lord God is the creator of heaven and earth.

In Isaiah 37:16,

O Lord of hosts, the God of Israel, who is enthroned
above the cherubim, You are the God, You alone, of all the
kingdoms of the earth. You have made heaven and earth.

Jesus is the only begotten Son of God.

In John 3:16,

> For God so loved the world, that he gave his only
> begotten Son, that whosoever believes in Him
> should not perish, but have everlasting life.

In John 1:14

> And the Word became flesh and dwelt among us,
> and we have seen his glory, glory as of the only Son
> from the Father, full of grace and truth.

The spirit of God: The Holy Spirit

In John 14:26,

> But the Helper, the Holy Spirit, whom the Father will
> send in my name, he will teach you all things and bring
> to your remembrance all that I have said to you.

Jesus died on the Cross, and His body was placed in the tomb
as was the custom following death.
In Mark 15:42–47,

And now when the evening was come and the preparation that is
the day before the Sabbath Joseph of Arimathaea, an honorable
counselor which also wait for the Kingdom of God came, and
went boldly to Pilate and craved the body of Jesus, and Pilate
marveled if He Jesus were already dead (as it normally took
more than several days for someone to die on a cross. As Jesus
had been on the cross six hours, with Pilate being skeptical) and
calling unto him his Centurion, he asked him whether HE had
been any while dead? And when he knew it of thee Centurion
he gave the body to Joseph. And he bought fine linen and took

him down from the Cross and wrapped Him in the linen and
laid Him in a sepulcher which had been hewn out of rock,
and rolled a stone unto the door of the sepulcher And Mary
Magdalene and the mother of Joseph beheld where He was laid.

The account of this event is chronicled in the book of Mark,
beginning in Mark 15:33–41.

I encourage you to take a few hours to read the Gospel accounts
of the crucifixion of Jesus as laid out on the following page. They
are all slightly different accounts of the same story. I was surprised I
preferred one written account over another. Blended all together, you
will find a total account of the immensity of that day when Jesus laid
down His life to conquer the powers of hell.

Scholars believe *Matthew's* Gospel was the first to be written. He
was a Jewish tax collector for the Roman Empire before his conversion to Christ.

Mark was Peter's protégé who helped Peter with his Greek language. The book of Mark was written shortly before the book of
Luke. Mark wrote the words of Peter, and his target audience were
the Roman Christians.

In Mark 14:51–52,

And a young man followed Jesus with nothing but
a linen loin cloth about his body; and they seized
him but he left the cloth and ran away naked.

Biblical scholars have placed that linen cloth within the social
artifacts, suggesting Mark was a person of wealthy means.

Luke is the beloved physician and a non-Jew. Luke writes of Jesus's
ministry as compassionate care with Jesus providing care for the mar-
ginalized and oppressed.

Apostle John was the disciple of John the Baptist, and then he
joined Jesus as a disciple being "the beloved" disciple. John and his
brother James were called Sons of Thunder by Jesus based on their
zeal, and they were the cousins of Jesus along the maternal line. John
witnessed the agony of Gethsemane at the foot at the Mount of

Olives in the garden raid when Jesus was arrested, the same night when Peter cut off the ear of a Roman guard in the scuffle.

In John 18:10,

Then Simon Peter, who had a sword, drew it and struck the high priest's servant [The man named Malchus], cutting off his right ear.

John was also only one of the three who witnessed the transfiguration of Christ after He ascended.

You may want to assemble a few pieces of lined paper on which to write the scriptures. There will be seventeen to twenty-four verses in each sampling for you to consider. You may use the indicated area on this page to capture highlights of each Gospel sampling.

The following are the verses: *Matthew 27:32–56, Mark 15:21–38, Luke 23:26–49*, and *John 19:16–37*. I encourage you to look in your Bible and record the verses from the Bible all written by those who loved the savior. You will be touched at the lens through which each writer captures their observations and heartache.

Matthew 27:32–56

____

____

____

____

Mark 15:21–38

____

____

____

____

Luke 23:26–49

____

____

____

____

John 19:16–37

____

____

____

____

Ten Books from the Christian Bookstore

I was a year beyond my illness and treatment. Still a slave to a medical opinion but free in my mind, or so I thought. I lost something in the interaction. I needed to find myself. I was saved from the jaws of death and was thankful. Pulling myself together or finding the missing puzzle pieces, I went to Florida where a warehouse bookstore was located. I packed my suitcase with ten books written by biblical scholars, preachers of all denominations, and a biblical word study. I felt confident I could find God in these books.

After reading all the books three weeks later, I was like a person who gets new glasses, but the lens' prescription in the frame is not correct. The person can see but not clearly.

How could I find what I was looking for?

But seek first his kingdom and his righteousness, and all these things will be given to you as well. (Matthew 6:33)

Walmart on a Summer Day

As I parked at the east end of the Walmart parking lot, a man in a black SUV pulled in next to me on my driver's side. This is the Walmart I frequently go to. I know some of the staff from my routine shopping habits. The man and I exited our cars at the same time. As he walked toward the store, I noted how his well-groomed hair shone brightly in the sun. I walked quickly as is my habit. I drew closer to the man as we entered the external doors into the store.

I sensed anger. Was this man in front of me blazing with anger? I suddenly became concerned for the greeter. The greater was a sweet Hispanic lady, and I saw her beginning to beam preparing to greet the customer before me. I saw the look on her face, and I knew my suspicion was spot-on. I flew past her. I met the man at the carting area. Our eyes met. "Good morning! What a lovey day! I hope you enjoy the day today, sir." And I smiled.

I took a cart and headed toward groceries, and I saw the man as he went back to the greeter. I prayed all the way to the mustard aisle. When I checked out, she was still at the greeting post. I hopped over the partition. "Did he apologize to you?"

"He did, and I told him I appreciated so that he took time to correct a wrong and that he made my day, and it was only nine o'clock."

We hugged. She was a champion and, I told her so.

These things that I have spoken to you, that my joy might remain with you, and that your joy might be filled. (John 15:11)

In Romans 14:17,

For the Kingdom of God is not eating and drinking, but righteousness and peace and joy in the Holy Spirit.

In Ephesians 1:17,

That the God of our Lord Jesus Christ, the Father of glory, may give unto you the Spirit of wisdom and Revelation in the knowledge in him.

We have learned that the Godhead is a triune of three: The Father, the Son, and the Holy Ghost.

Sadly, it's like someone who has three siblings and invites all over for a meal and yet talks to only two of the three. We would call that rude. Scores of churches do it all the time. People do it all the time, ignoring the Spirit of God.

We will never draw near to God by ignoring the Spirit.

In John 16:13–15,

> He will bring glory to me by taking from what is mine
> and making it known to you. All that belongs to the
> Father is mine. That is why I said the Spirit will take
> that what is mine and make it known to you.

I have heard many stories of people outside of America who, after reading the book of John in the Bible, became immediately saved. John was the closest disciple to Jesus.

As Jesus's ministry began to gain momentum, He took on twelve disciples. These twelve is the inner circle. The Spirit of God, the Holy Spirit, was active in Jesus's life. There is little evidence that the disciples had a working relationship with the Holy Spirit as they ministered with Jesus, hence Jesus saying, "I will leave and then the Comforter will come."

I do believe John had extraordinary understanding if not for being an apostle to John the Baptist who had a large ministry ahead of that of Jesus. John the Apostle was considered a pillar of the new church. John being close in age to Jesus was the only disciple not martyred but died of natural causes a few years after writing the Book of Revelation.

Luke did not have a personal relationship with Jesus. He was a disciple in a greater sense following the death of Jesus. Luke gained his knowledge from Paul who taught him the Bible. It is believed Luke got the story of Jesus's birth and death directly from Mary.

Paul was a Roman, and Luke was a Gentile.

The Gospels of Luke and John both say that Satan "entered" Judas at certain times and may have influenced his decision to betray Jesus. Jesus speaks in John 17:12. These verses are from the NIV Bible (The New International Bible).

In Luke 22:1–6,

> Now the Feast of Unleavened Bread, called the Passover, was
> approaching, and the chief priests and the teachers of the law
> were looking for some way to get rid of Jesus, for they were

afraid of the people. Then Satan entered Judas, called Iscariot, one of the Twelve. And Judas went to the chief priests and the officers of the temple guard and discussed with them how he might betray Jesus. They were delighted and agreed to give him money. He consented, and watched for an opportunity to hand Jesus over to them when no crowd was present.

In John 17:12,

While I was with them, I protected them and kept them safe by that name you gave me. None has been lost except the one doomed to destruction so that Scripture would be fulfilled.

The Gospel of John describes Judas as an untrustworthy person. It claims that Judas was the treasurer for Jesus and His twelve disciples, carrying the money bag the group shared and sometimes stealing from it. When a woman put perfume on Jesus shortly before the last supper, Judas objected. The Gospel of John says,

Why wasn't this perfume sold and the money given to the poor? It was worth a year's wages.' He did not say this because he cared about the poor, but because he was a thief; as keeper of the money bag, he used to help himself to what was put into it. (John 12:4–6)

But anyone who does not love does not know
God, for God is love. (1 John 4:8)

The Father God is love, and Jesus is the judge.
In Acts 10:42,

And He commanded us to preach to the people,
and to testify that it is He who was ordained by
God to be Judge of the living and the dead.

The Spirit of God is wisdom

In James 1:5,

If any of you lacks wisdom, you should ask God, who gives generously to all without finding fault, and it will be given to you.

In Ephesians 1:17–18,

That the God of our Lord Jesus Christ the Father of Glory may give unto you the Spirit of Wisdom and Revelation in the knowledge of Him; The eyes of your understanding being enlightened that you may know the hope of His calling and what the riches of the glory of His inheritance in the Saints.

The Spirit of God is might

In Isaiah 40:29,

He gives strength to the weary and increases the power of the weak.

The Spirit of God is grace

In 2 Timothy 2:1–2,

You therefore, my son, be strong in the grace that is in Christ Jesus. The things which you have heard from me in the presence of many witnesses, entrust these to faithful men who will be able to teach others also.

The Spirit of God is truth

In John 16:3–4,

When the Spirit of truth comes, he will guide you into all truth, for he will not speak on his own authority, but whatever he hears, he will speak, and he will declare to you the things that are to come.

CHAPTER 5

God in You

Walmart's Book Section

IT WAS ANOTHER grocery run today. I was on my third nursing job. Things could be better, but this is life. I was working at an emergent call center. It was a fast-paced job, and I felt it suited me. I read a lot of books, all with Christian leanings. One of those books was titled *Heaven is for Real*, about a pastor's young son who was killed in an accident and revived. The entire book is about the child's trip to heaven.

I am standing at the Walmart book aisle, noticing they weren't publishing books fast enough for me to read, not books offered for sale by Walmart anyway.

There was a new book with a boy in a wheelchair on the cover. I have been in the room when a miracle happens. I realized part of my desire to work where the lines of life and death run so closely parallel was that I could often sense a stronger presence of God in those times, offering a different reality than what may be in the room. My understanding was that no one goes to heaven returning in the same condition because there is only perfection in heaven.

How could this book I viewed be claiming a trip to heaven and the boy on the cover in a wheelchair? I was struggling to understand. There was that voice again, and it said, "Look at the author's name."

I did. Alex and Kevin Malarkey were the authors.

That immediately solved my dilemma. I began praying in earnest for the boy and his family, praying that God would make Himself known and help them with whatever they needed. I know that tragedy, the type where the patient survives, almost always places an undiscernible burden on the entire family system. In 2015, the boy publicly stated the fallacy of his story, and I prayed for them again that they would find God's love and provision.

> Nevertheless, I tell you the truth: It is expedient for you that I
> go away: for if I go not away, the Comforter will not come to
> you: but if I depart, I will send him unto you. (John 16:7)

I was in a healing prayer service where a tall black man was concerned about chest pain that had cropped up. I was in the second-row pew, and as they prayed for the man, I saw a stationary tub as water splashed in the tub. The frayed edges on the hard plastic drain plug let water leak through. I immediately thought that indicated a possible valve problem and knew that it should not wait. I told the ministers who informed the man's wife, and they went to the ED as the man was having pain.

As you become more aware of the ways of God and the Holy Spirit, your friends or work partners might be the first to notice the change in you. God will also open up new friendships, and your life will feel like you are in a canoe, gently drifting downstream.

I did not realize the strength of my own will. I have a sweet personality, and I love to have fun, but I was shocked at the force with which I plowed headfirst into life.

My healthcare industry was changing, and as someone who loves to work, I was finding my work life, providing most of the angst in my life. I turned my work life over to God. I essentially said, "I would work where you send me."

My resume is a divine work of art.

While this was going on, I understood to a greater degree that giving to the works of God was critical. Jesus, with all He was able to do, the Bible tells us they took alms or money. Jesus and the disciples used money with miracles to accomplish the necessary things.

You will feel a nudge to give. I have given varying amounts of money and, more than once, a month's wage to a cause God made known. I have learned to deny myself. Self-deprivation is a voluntary choice.

My newest job was at an organization that helps those with disabilities. I met Mr. Little at a small corporate event. When I met him, I heard from the voice that his name was Little, but he was huge in the Spirit. I told him those exact words. My, how he laughed. I loved his laugh; it was so genuine. A few months later, I was working with his team. He and I talked about various topics, and when the subject of tithing came up, he told me this story.

My wife and I were visiting a church away from home. A minister from Africa was there as a speaker. I liked what the man had to say. I heard I should give an offering to this man. Of course, I will.

He told me he and his wife had a savings account as married couples. Those funds usually are earmarked for some future purpose. I was responsible for my resources, and I recognized that I had only to decide the direction of my tithing. It was my choice alone. I realized his situation was different. I was feeling for his wife as he told me this story.

He continued.

So I said, "Yes, of course. I will." And I was thinking of numbers in my head.

God budged in and said, "Give what you have in your savings account."

"Wait, God, that's her account too."

"Well, ask her."

Mr. Little sitting with his wife in the second row of pews in the front of the church leaned over as the minister was speaking and whispered to his wife that God had said they would give an offering to the visiting minister. "Of course," was her reply.

He sat for a moment to think of how to tell her what he had heard.

God said to give him our savings account.

Give it all to this man? Flew out of her mouth.

He told me they got home at midnight. They wrote the check and put it in a stamped envelope and the mailbox before 1:00 a.m.

I prayed for him for years. He was heading in the right direction.

I remember the first time I wrote a big check for God's work. I felt victorious somehow that heaven was aware of my voluntary self-mastery.

I'm telling you this because this is how the kingdom of God works with miracles and money.

CHAPTER 6

Prophesy

PROPHECY FIRST IS shown in the Bible in Deuteronomy 28:18–19, written 1451 during the time of the priests and Levites.

The Levite tribe was vested with keeping the holy things of God. Animal offerings were customary, oxen and ram primarily. This is foreshadowed of Christ who would die on the cross for our sins. There were specific ways in which offerings should be offered, and there existed laws for the priests. It is here that the first fruits are discussed as being the portion that the people give to priests and the sanctuary.

Deuteronomy chapter 18 is a good place to start reading to understand the dedication of the Levites to God. The first word that God gives regarding prophecy is found in the Book of Deuteronomy.

In Deuteronomy 18:18–19,

> I will raise then up a Prophet from amongst their brethren, like
> unto you, and will put My Words into his mouth, and He shall
> speak unto them; all the I shall command him. And it shall
> come to pass that to whomever will not harken unto My Words
> which he will speak in My Name, I will require it of him.

In the Old Testament, the book of 1 Kings is where the prophet Elijah is first made known in 900 BC.

Elijah's name means "God is Jehovah." He is considered one of the greatest prophets, and he was brought into the Bible story by the Holy Spirit without fanfare and/or introduction. A prophecy was the tool created by God to foretell Christ's birth and death.

In 1 Kings 17:1,

> And Elijah the Tishbite, who was of the inhabitations
> of Gilead said unto Ahab. As the Lord God of Israel
> lives, before Whom I stand, there shall be not one drop
> of dew nor rain these years according to my word.

In 1 Kings 17:2–5,

> And then the word of the Lord came unto him, saying Get you hence and turn eastward and hide yourself by the brook Cherith, that is before Jordan and it shall be that you shall drink from the brook: and I have commanded the ravens to feed you there. So he went and did according unto the word of the LORD; for he went and dwelt by the brook Cherith, this is before Jordan.

You will want to read the entire chapter 17 of 1 Kings to understand the purpose of prophecy. Prophecy is one of the gifts of the Spirit.

1 Corinthians 12:8–10 lists the Spiritual gifts.

These are the gifts of the Spirit according to the King James Bible—charismatic gifts:

1. *The word of knowledge*
2. *Increased faith*
3. *The gifts of healing*
4. *The gift of miracles*
5. *Prophecy*
6. *The discernment of spirits*
7. *Diverse kinds of tongues*
8. *Interpretation of tongues*

There are many prophets in the world; some are more well-known than others. Kim Clement of Destiny House was such a prophet. I had the pleasure of seeing him before his death in 2016. There are many YouTube videos that the family put out as they have taken the responsibility to keep their father's words available for believers.

Prophetic words are often referred to as timeless. Timeless because God Himself transcends time.

In Matthew 10:41

The ones who receives a prophet because he is a prophet
will receive a prophet's reward, and the one who
receives a righteous person because he is a righteous
person will receive a righteous person's reward.

Prophets are a part of the fivefold ministry of Christ: apostles, prophets, evangelists, shepherds (pastors), and teachers.

When I think of the prophetic gifts, I think of grace.

In Colossians 1:9–10,

For this cause we also, since the day we heard of it, do not
cease to pray for you and your desire that you might be
filled with the knowledge of His will That you might walk
worthy of the Lord unto all pleasing, being fruitful in every
good work and increasing in the knowledge of God.

I love the book of Colossians, which is the gospel of Paul. I suggest you read the first chapter of the book of Colossians or the entire book, which has a few chapters. I can picture Paul standing and preaching to the people with direct and rich words, all as a testimony to the greatness of God who saved his soul from the pit of hell. Paul is ever mindful of his life with Christ as a superior choice.

Have you ever heard the testimony of an ex-drug abuser who came off drugs? Passionate. Their testimony is so powerful to celebrate their claim of newfound truth. The actual being that life is far grander when a body and mind are not addicted to drugs.

The Old Testament in 1 Kings cried out the warning of false prophets. Of course, untrue things are everywhere, and you have false prophets online; you will discern the darkness of the untruth as they speak, and you will shun the voice. That is if you know how to discern the difference. How will you know the difference? The Spirit of God in you, once saved, will tune your ear to many things for your knowledge.

For example, a minister with a subtitled event with large followers had a livestreamed evangelical event. I was skeptical for reasons unknown. Thirty minutes into the livestream, a close-up of the man's fingernails bitten down to the quick with bloody edges as he handheld the microphone. I could see why my spirit could not receive the word with my ears. You have a choice to make; choose truth as your standard. Choose to be on the side of light. A laissez-faire attitude with untruth is a slippery slope to darkness. You can see by the revolution of the world's peoples that they are fighting an unseen force. It is a force that subverts truth and eliminates freedom. I wonder who would be doing that?

In Ephesians 6:12,

> For we wrestle not against flesh and blood, but principalities,
> against powers, against the rulers of the darkness of this
> world, against spiritual wickedness in high places.

The prophetic voice has been shunned by the current mainstream church, which is a total disservice in my opinion. As church leaders, one should be educating and equipping the saints to enhance discernment and knowledge. Let the people hear for themselves their own ears able to discern truth from untruth.

In Acts 2:17,

> And it shall come to pass In the last days, saith God, I will
> pour out my Spirit on all people; your sons and daughters will
> prophesy, your young men will see visions, your old men will
> dream dreams. And on my servants and on my handmaidens I
> will pour out in those days My Spirt and they shall prophesy.

There was a point in time as I worked in Psych, when I had ample vacation time. This was when God sent me to churches to see, hear, and learn. As a nurse, I have great comfort in asking difficult questions. I do not judge, and that is what helped me help my patients as best I could. I was in North Carolina at a three-day ministry event. It was in the church Rick Joyner refurbished after it had been used by another ministry. People from all over the Eastern United States predominantly worked with the restoration project. I met a man originally from Russia. It is strange that I have encountered several Russian men in my tours chasing God.

This man had angelic help fleeing from Russia. We will call him Seth. Seth heard the word while at a coffee shop. *Pack one suitcase and be at the northwest corner from your house, and a man in a white car will pick you and your family up.* Seth knew his life was threatened. He worked in a drug ring. He was a senior man in the ring. He did not receive the word from who I assume was a prophetic voice in the coffee shop.

As he sat at a stoplight the next day as he drove to work. Someone hopped in his front seat. He thought that door was locked. The man said something to the effect. "What is your name?"

Seth was so shocked and still thinking how did this man enter his passenger seat and told him his real name. He couldn't believe he did that.

The man went on to say God had made a way for him to escape the lie he was living. Seth said he wasn't interested.

The man said, "Your young daughter who you love will be taken if you don't obey. Pack one bag." He repeated the block to the north pickup at 7:00 a.m. The man immediately left the car at the next stoplight.

Seth went on to tell me he had since repented to God for his response, and he was working off what he owed God at the restoration project. I hugged him and told him how proud I was of him, and his face turned pink.

I met a man who had been encountered by God as he sat on the toilet in the men's room at an airport. It had to do with a phone call the man had made a few hours prior. He made a call to correct a wrong after exiting the men's lounge. I heard a few other bathroom stories and thought what a sense of humor God has.

I also had my own epiphany of my delight at being made female. This was not the first story I heard of a man fighting against the will of God.

Another cold November night

Believe it or not, there were days when I had two hours' notice to get dressed and be somewhere. God knew my work schedule, and of course, once I turned over my work life to Him, what did I expect?

The guest speaker was at a central house of worship, which I rarely attended. He was a thin man with dark-brown eyes. He said a prophet was coming to the church he attended. He did not sign up for ministry time with the prophet. He knew about it, and he had decided he wasn't letting God or anyone screw up his retirement plan. The event he described occurred in his last several months as an employee.

John said he worked in the building industry. He is a foreman. It was a few days before Christmas, and it was payday. He had the pleasure of taking the checks to the employees, wishing them a blessed holiday. There were three active projects sites, and he decided to start with the one farthest from home.

The third site was a new church building, a brand-new structure. As he pulled into the place, the crane was setting in the third-floor rafters. As he walked to the foreman at the sight, the foreman said he would like to hand out the checks to his men. It was agreed, and John decided to go up and assist the crane operator place the beams. He could do this in his sleep; he has done it many times.

He went up to the third floor, and he didn't know what had happened, but the structure gave way, and he tumbled three stories through the air. If you have ever seen a new construction plan for a bathroom, two copper pipes stand vertical before the toilet piece is affixed.

He said he broke eighty-two bones. The two copper pipes skewered his body, breaking big bones and tiny bones as his body slammed into the unfinished bathroom. He lived in a body cast for a long time.

I was delighted I was not sitting in my customary second row. I was in the eighth pew row when I let out a momentous laugh. A laugh I think only God understood.

That night was the kingpin of the men in the bathroom teaching series, and it was worthy of a grand tithe.

From the mouth of a child

The absolute sweetest prophetic word I ever had was from a six-year-old. The boy was jumping up and down with excitement, and the adorable round-faced black boy with dreadlocks gave the word: "Lady, you're a lady, and you are on fire. Lady, you are on fire, and the Holy Spirit is squeezing you and squeezing you. HE is squeezing you tight. Boy, lady, you're on fire."

It took me about six months to find the meaning of that word. That God would let it flow from the mouth of a babe made it my most favored word. The word meant VBAC.

As the body of Christ, the prophetic times before us is greater than those behind. We must free up the prophetic voices and embrace their function of accomplishing the work of the later-day church.

CHAPTER 7

A Just God

THE PEOPLE OF the world are protesting the thievery of their freedoms. Governments that shun truth work to bring deception and division are not of God. I saw a YouTube of a young woman speaking out in New York City. Her voice was a clarion call to parents, siblings, neighbors, and the church. When you listen to charismatic people, it is good they refer to God. That alone is not the positive litmus test for but taken in with visual clues, not dressed in Madison Fifth-Avenue suits nor rags; these prolific speakers have worked somewhere where they have seen the corrupt removal of guidelines and accountability from their institutions. Hate speech, lies, and tyrannical actions should give each one of us a pause. We should ask God what we should pray and do? How, Dear Lord, can I help your plan for my country?

I posed the question to five friends as we sat sipping coffee. What do you think could happen if, at noon on Sunday, all of God's children around the world prayed to God? Do you think He would answer? Do you think He would act?

We all agreed. Yes, those things would happen. Prayer works.

In John 10:10 (NIV),

> The thief comes only to steal and kill and destroy; I have
> come that they may have life, and have it to the full.

44

There are sixty-three verses referring to darkness to light in the Bible. Here are a few examples:
In John 1:5,

> The light shines in the darkness, and the
> darkness comprehend it not.

In John 8:12,

> Then spoke Jesus again to them, saying, I am the
> light of the world. Whoever follows me shall not walk
> in darkness, but shall have the light of life.

In Psalm 119:105,

> Your word is a lamp unto my feet and a light unto my path.

In 2 Corinthians 4:6,

> For God, who commanded the light to shine out of
> darkness," has shined in our hearts to give the light of the
> knowledge of the glory of God, the face of Jesus Christ.

In Proverbs 4:18–19,

> But the path of the just is like the light of dawn, which shines
> more and more until the perfect day. The way of the wicked
> is as darkness; they know not at what they stumble.

I have always loved boys. Please don't ask me why. This story is for all you mothers who have sons.

A warm Southern night

I was down south on another trip suggested by God. I was sitting next to a recovered drug addict, a man a few years younger than me; he had been addicted since eighteen years of age: everything, including crack.

He lost track of the ED's he had been in. Nonjudgement is the rule in health care. Judgment kills the ability to be compassionate, which goes out the window. It's the goal for every health care and EMS worker in the United States and, I believe, globally as well.

Overdosing is never the goal for a drug user; pain management is often sought for emotional pain. The liver bears all the brunt of a drug overdose. If your body isn't up to the massive detox effort ahead, it will shut down the system.

Prisoners must receive bread and water daily because, without such, the walls of the gut begin folding in on itself, and the heart starts to fire infarcts, infarcts to take the heart of the body out of what is a death of pure agony.

The Chinese that do organ harvesting is such agony. When I heard a US Army General describe the process, the nurse in me ran to the toilet and heaved.

I asked this man with jet-black hair, fair complexion, and hazel eyes what he knew about God? He got teary-eyed. He knew very well, he said. He went on to tell that it was his last overdose that pushed his body to a grinding halt. He said he was quasi-saved, whatever that is. He said as he stood before Jesus, knowing he could get into heaven; he was pretty sure.

Jesus called him by his name and said he could not be allowed into heaven, as the man said a silent prayer renewing his belief in God. Jesus stepped aside, and like looking into the top of a snow globe, as this man looked through the floor, he saw a woman kneeling at a bedside. "Do you know this woman?" Jesus asked.

"It's my mother," he said.

"Yes, that is your mother, and because of her prayers, you must return."

With that, his heart monitor picked up a normal sinus rhythm. In Isaiah 43:10,

> You are my witnesses, says the LORD, and my servant
> whom I have chosen, that you may know and believe

me and understand that I am He. Before me no god
was formed, nor shall there be any after Me.

In John 15:16,

You have not chosen Me but I have chosen you.

In Ephesians 2:8–9,

For by grace are you saved through faith; and that not of yourselves;
it is a gift from God. Not of works least any man boast. For we
are his workmanship, created in Christ Jesus unto good works
which God has before ordained that we should walk in them.

The church today must be of one accord. We must recognize
the enemy and know we have the power through Christ to wage a
war. The blood of Christ foretells the victory at hand.
In Acts 26:16–18,

But rise and stand upon your feet, for I have appeared to you
for this purpose, to make you a minster and witness to the
things in which you have seen me and to those in which I will
appear to you, delivering you from your people and from the
Gentiles—to whom I am sending you to open their eyes, so
that they may turn from darkness to light and from the power
of Satan to God, that they may receive forgiveness of sins
and a place among those who are sanctified by faith in me

This is the call God is giving believers today. Rise and stand.
Get a fresh presence of the Almighty in your life. Moses knew he
needed the presence of God, and John's writings say much about the
anointing of God.
In Psalm 45:7,

You love righteousness, and hate wickedness; therefore God, your
God has anointed you with the oil of gladness above you fellows

Faith is not a competition; it is a calling. God equips the saints. The new convert has fire and momentum, and the rest of us have wisdom and experience with God. Dust off your Bible and shake complacency from your inner parts. Join a new church if yours is not teaching power teachings appropriate to the time in which we live. If you are in a church saying rapture is close, I remind you that the scriptures say all the world needs to hear the gospel, then the end will come.

In Matthew 24:14,

> And this gospel of the kingdom shall be preached in all the world
> for a witness unto all nations; and then shall the end come.

There is much work to be done. It looks doubtful a return to the world as we knew it will occur. A new normal is upon us. Satan and those who follow his edicts are not slowing down in their drive to push a reality onto us that is void of freedom, truth, and independence. We all need to be hearing from God. And we must belong to like-minded people groups who believe in the same God and have the same understanding as laid out by Christ and the first church. There are one hundred Bible verses on the power of the word.

In Romans 10:17,

> So faith comes from hearing, and hearing
> through the word of Christ.

In Acts 20:32,

> And now I commend you to God and to the word of
> his grace, which is able to build you up and to give you
> the inheritance among all those who are sanctified.

In Isaiah 40:8,

> The grass withers, the flower fades, but the
> word of our God will stand forever.

In Colossians 3:16,

Let the word of Christ dwell in you richly in all wisdom;
teaching and admonishing one another in psalms and hymns and
spiritual songs, singing with grace in your hearts to the Lord.

In Romans 12:4–5,

For as we have many members in one body, and all members
have not the same office: So we, being many, are one
body in Christ, and every one members one of another.
Whatever is true for one is also true for the other.

In John 1:1–5,

In the beginning was the Word, and the Word was with
God, and the Word was God. The same was in the beginning
with God. And all things were made by Him, and without
him was not anything made that was made. In Him was
life, and the life was the light of men. The light shines in
the darkness, and the darkness comprehended it not.

In Matthew 18:20,

For where two or three are gathered together in
my name, there am I in the midst of them.

In Ephesians 3:20–21,

Let the word of Christ dwell in you richly in all wisdom;
teaching and admonishing one another in psalms and hymns and
spiritual songs, singing with grace in your hearts to the Lord.

Heaven's rear gate

I have tithed to missions since working my first job at the age of fifteen. My family tithed to missions. Linguists entered the field before the missionaries many times. There are cultures where "to carry" may not be in the vocabulary. The linguist would create a word to impart the cultural language's meaning.

In Orlando, Florida, there are Wycliffe Translators. Their mission is Bible translation. The bookshop is worth the trip to Wycliffe. The stories written by missionaries are many of the best books I have read.

Let me tell you what happened the day that I was there. As you walk into a large building, there is a gallery of wax figures along the wall. There are no identifiers on them; they are in traditional clothing, and that is the only way you could discern their origin.

The teaching tools along the wall explain that the new birth of mission location is a secret for safety reasons.

As I stood admiring the wax figures dressed in stunning weaved outfits, a group of six people, three men and three women, walked in. They went up to the wax replicas and started naming them, commenting on how well the wax characterization fits the natural person.

I asked if they were linguists. Yes, they were. Were they a team? "More or less" was the answer.

I still had no clue about the origin of the people the figurines represented.

I then went to lunch at a local Chinese restaurant. A lovely young woman came to the table. I could see she is not Chinese as I looked at her beautiful face. She came to America, leaving her husband and two children home. I asked where home was. She told me, and I realized she was from the place the linguists I had just met had most likely been. I prayed that those six linguists would follow my lead to the Chinese restaurant and find my waitress. What a joyful event that would be.

I was in a church in Florida. It was not a big church, yet it held many people. I did not know who would be speaking. God had told me three weeks prior I needed to get here.

The man on the stage had a presence about him. I could tell by the look on his face he had a confession. My heart went out to him. He ran a mission, and I had tithed to that mission. The guest speaker began:

"I ran a big mission, know how to run missions, and run excellent missions. I had a medical condition that took me to heaven. The line to Jesus was long. I wandered out of the line. It was not manicured surroundings; I saw no gold streets. I heard a noise like pans clinking or something, and I followed the sound. I came to a back gate. There were plant pots and things you would see around a gardener's dwelling. Is this heaven? Where is the front door?

"I yelled for some attention. 'Hey, anyone there? Is anyone there?' This is so and so. You know me. I run missions. I run big missions for you.

"A moment of silence.

"'You said you run big missions for me?'

"'Yes, for you. Who else would I do it for?'

"This banter went back and forth for several minutes, and you could hear both sides, and yet I heard God's side the clearest. When you are the one in the hot seat, I have heard that your ears stop working, and the mouth goes into overdrive. The mouth of so and so was going into overdrive.

"And then a beefsteak tomato came sailing over the wall and hit so and so square in the face. Why was he being treated this way? He was demoralized and in disbelief. Yet, he knew God never lies. He didn't understand how he could do massive grand missions and not be doing it for God. Then he had a realization, and there was only one thing to do. So he offered God a deal. 'I know what you say is accurate, and if You allow me to go back, I will do missions, not for myself, but You alone.'"

He received a standing ovation, and he was a champion of the faith.

If you pastor a flock, this story may have significance for you in some way. The message of this story is, it is never too late to change your course and get back to doing the work God has for you to do. You are a champion of your faith!

In Matthew 6:23,

But if your eye is evil, your whole body will be full of darkness. If, therefore, the light in you is darkness, how great is the darkness!

In John 1:3–5,

All things were made by Him and without Him, was not anything made that was made. In Him was life and the life was the light of men, And the light shines in the darkness, and the darkness comprehends It not.

CHAPTER 8

Shine Your Light

A fall carnival

I WAS HELPING a friend who had set up a craft booth at the carnival grounds the night before. The weather report was perfect for such a fun event. The following morning the tent top was crumpled in a heap upon arriving at the tent site. A storm had swirled through, hitting some of the crafter's overhead structures. I sensed a demonic presence was responsible. As the event got underway—there were several crafters at nearby sites and a gambling table with scratch-off cards three doors down.

As I sat on a stool, six teenage boys approached me. Small talk began, and then one of them asked me if I was a Christian. I mentioned in the affirmative my senses heightened. They were pretty aggressive in their questions and not mere curiosity for their age.

One asked, "So you hear from God? [I never said I did]. Can you tell us what numbers to pick to win money at the booth over there?"

I told them gambling is a Satanic endeavor. God is not against anyone winning money; however, the 10 percent rule always applies, and if you want to score points with God Almighty, you could give 25 percent of your winnings, that is, if you should win.

They were visibly excited as I stood wondering. What terrible kind of situation had I created?

My mouth flew open, and numbers flew out for about eight seconds. I had never been so glad to shut my mouth ever.

The boys were crowding the gambling booth, and it took three minutes until I heard cheers, and they were heading toward me.

"Oh, this is real. It's really real," the one boy said.

"God is authentic," I said.

I was dumbstruck, and the boys were thrilled. They asked where they should give their 10 percent, and one asked about giving his 25 percent. I imagined he would be a pastor someday or, at the very least, a benefactor of God's work.

I could not wait for the vendor table to close. I was not at ease on the inside. Once I got my car and went home, I began repenting to God, and I was way out of my comfort zone. How close to scripture was that interaction?

The voice said, "You just saved six boys who were one step away from indoctrination into a Satanic camp. Job well done."

I prayed for those boys for months that they would find God sooner rather than later and that the darkness would repulse them.

In Psalm 25:8–10,

Good and upright is the Lord: therefore will he teach sinners
in the way. The meek will he guide in judgment: and the meek
will he teach his way. All the paths of the Lord are mercy and
truth unto such as keep his covenant and his testimonies.

In Psalm 32:7–8,

Thou art my hiding place; thou shalt preserve me from trouble;
thou shalt compass me about with songs of deliverance.
Selah. 8 I will instruct thee and teach thee in the way
which thou shalt go: I will guide thee with mine eye.

In Luke 4:33–35,

> In the Synagogue there was a man. Which had a Spirit of an unclean devil, And cried out with aloud voice: Saying let us alone What have we to do with You thou Jesus of Nazareth.? Are you come to destroy us? I know who you are the Holy One, of God. 25 And Jesus rebuked him saying Hold Your peace and come out of him. And when the devil had thrown the man down, he came out of him, and hurt him not.

I have been to several church services away from my home state. It was in these places I realized about deliverance. I pray the churches will embrace this critical move of the spirit to set the captives free. Satan has many tools in his tool kit to get a person to join his dark minion. Sexual sin is the biggest tool in the box. Sexual sin is pornography, infidelity, sex outside of marriage, and so much more.

Christians must be ever mindful of their actions that they do not open the door to Satan's meddling. Of course, there are times when five deliverance ministers together will break the demonic hold in people. You see, these people today as photographed by the Border Police. Humans with animalistic behaviors caught on camera at the Texas border are the smugglers. That is the most overt character of a possessed individual.

There is a need for deliverance far and wide in the church. Seriously injured car accident victims, crime survivors, rape, and other abusive acts perpetrated on people. Bill and Beni Johnson at Bethel Church understand the need for deliverance as do other preachers worldwide. The passage above tells us that it was a synagogue member who Jesus delivered. I believe deliverance is the most abundant form of God's love, and we mustn't make a mistake for judging it for something it is not.

Once you have Christ on the inside of you, the best way to get some deliverance from things you are not aware of is to say, "God, Here I am. Use me. Jesus, use me." Strongholds are in our minds. The renewing of our minds is the remedy according to scripture.

I would wake up, and my mind would be changed. Sometimes big changes and others not so much, and I always thanked God for the work He had done to renew my mind. Once, I was framed, and it cost me my job. That one offense took a lot to break the stronghold associated with it. I found myself waking up praying for the person responsible.

When I was fighting for my healing, I knew I must forgive everyone if I expected God to heal me. I put six names on the list and prayed to God to release the unforgiveness I have on them and bless them with the knowledge of Christ.

As I sat in the middle of the row of the American flight headed to San Francisco, I once again prayed for the six on the list. I did not know if I had unforgiveness, but I came to believe that with God, anything is possible. As I sat praying, she popped visually into my mind. I met her in sixth grade. She had red hair. I have the gift of hospitality, which was evident in my childhood. This girl loved the parties I set up. That part made me happy. Her actions did not fall in line with her vocalizations, and she would run around the table and knock off six or eight cookies before the party started and eat with joy. I remembered talking to my mom more than once about this problem. I could take a special box of cookies just for her. That, to me, seemed unfair to everyone else. Then live with it and don't get so mad was the advice.

This girl should have been on my list as the seventh person. I laughed, and then I teared up. I felt horrible. Who was I to hold this against her, a child, my peer? I prayed for a long time for her, her family, her children, and that God would richly bless her. Maybe she ran a cookie bakeshop, and if she did, I prayed for good wholesome customers. I sincerely thanked God for helping me recognize the problem to correct it.

In 1 Corinthians 10:13,

There hath no temptation taken you but such as is common to man: but God is faithful, who will not suffer you to be

> tempted above that ye are able; but will with the temptation
> also make a way to escape, that ye may be able to bear it.

In Romans 12:2,

> And be not conformed to this world: but be ye transformed
> by the renewing of your mind, that ye may prove what is
> that good, and acceptable, and perfect, will of God.

3:00 a.m.

I had worked in psych for about five or six years. God, I know, gave me this job to get a good sense of the spiritual realm. I loved my job, and I loved my patients. How I tried to get them to see how very much God loved them and that the Holy Spirit was on their side all the way. I will be forever thankful for their ability to share their truth with me so that I may understand.

This job afforded me a lot of opportunities to travel and chase God. I have much respect for ER staff. They were gutsy, and I say that will all the love possible. It was sometimes difficult to discern the care needed as numerous people were usually hauled in by the police. Sometimes a drug addict gets sent to psych. That was never good. In psych, I realized that drug addiction was not my calling.

One late afternoon, the security brought in a man about thirty years of age. He was a grown man who, as an infant, laid on the umbilical cord during delivery, creating deficits. He lived with his parents, who adored him. His three brothers were all ministers.

The report was, he left the house prior as he had done before to go to the corner store just a few driveways away from his parents' house. When the man did not return home from his trip to the neighborhood store, his parents looked for him. They didn't have to look far as he laid on the sidewalk one driveway from his home, and he was suddenly mute.

I admitted him, and he remained mute. I sensed a very evil plot. I had a keen discernment for such things. The one brother followed me off the unit as I left as I had to be back at 3:00 a.m., which was then twelve hours away.

He told me his brother had encountered a prostitute. That is all I had to hear. This plot was aimed at one of the brothers and was the intended target to weaken his faith, and this stunt was Satan pushing his plan. All battles are spiritual battles. I told the brother. I asked if he knew any minister who did deliverance? He did not. I left for home, praying all the way. I had a mix of emotions I could not describe.

I went to bed and hardly slept. God showed me the face of the brother I knew who had some understanding of such things. I got up, showered dressed all nearly in my sleep as I drove back to work.

When I stepped on the unit, all the lights were on. All patients get many heavy sleeping aides, and it worked so well that the ice maker sounded like a foghorn on the unit at 3:00 a.m. I usually brought bags of ice or frozen drinks when I worked nights.

I unlocked the door and stepped into the unit. I could not discern the environment due to a lack of sleep.

The security guard said he came bolting out of his room at 2:00 a.m., frightful and scared, yelling, "They are coming to kill me. They are coming to kill me!" With that, the gentle giant collapsed in front of the med room door. My heart broke. I went to the funeral the next day. It was the most painful thing I had witnessed in a very long time.

In 1 Peter 5:8,

Be sober, be vigilant; because your adversary the devil, as a roaring lion, walketh about, seeking whom he may devour:

God showed me that the power of Satan through physical bonds that are not covered by the covenant bonds of marriage can be deadly. This was a setup. The purity of the gentle giant who now lay in the casket is as that of a child. Child trafficking or child abuse with the perversion of sexual sin is an awful thing I know of in a spiritual sense. We must and the church must stand against it. What will it take for us to be outraged at the atrocity of sin of this nature?

If you are in a committed marriage and feel drawn to foster parent, let this be your confirmation. These children have suffered greatly at the hands of demonic oppressors. The answer is a family that loves combined with the enveloping outer shell of a faith community. Pray to God and know that he will answer, offering much grace, it will blow you away.

In 1 Corinthians 13:13,

> And now abide faith, hope, love, these three;
> but the greatest of these is love.

A day like no other

I was home all alone. It was a brilliant sun-filled day. Birds were chirping with excitement over the new feed in the feeder. The bees were buzzing, getting the last pollen of the season. Yesterday, a 4.2-centimeter mass on my lower colon was discovered. I had become one serious organic vegan connoisseur years ago. I used distilled water, taking more vitamins than food most days. I had zero signs of any problem, but the thought had floated through my mind a few weeks prior. I imagined my first cancer treatment caused this anomaly. I worked with doctors every day. I was getting so much advice I could not register all of it, nor did I want to. God was going to have to fix this. I had made up my mind.

It was a crisp, clear autumn day. My mind was racing. I tried to remain calm, finding it impossible.

I stood in my back room that looked over the yard, the flowers of summer starting to fade. I cried out to God. "Dear God, if you are real, I need to know it. I need to know it now."

I hadn't even finished the sentence, and the room started to drip a thick honey substance from the walls. I was prostrated on the floor. The air was thick. Now I was sobbing. I felt something, and then I heard, "I Am God Almighty. Mighty and can do *all* things."

There was thunder in my house. My mind was stuck because I had no idea what the full definition of the word *all* was. All was too big of a word for me to comprehend. Then a movie reel flew before my eyes. I burst out sobbing again. I knew him immediately in his blue jeans and his yellow shirt and a blonde mop of hair on his head, and he was smiling. It was Timmy. He was like a brother and indeed my best friend. He was struck by a car and killed over thirty years prior. I had just a moment to realize he was in heaven. What a clown he was.

Then the movie reel went faster. One by one. All men. All my patients. Most of my patients didn't return when they coded or flatlined. And God said, "My commandments would keep anyone safe," and a red Traveler's insurance umbrella popped up in my view. "With My commandments, you may get a wound from the enemy Satan, but you will never get taken out. Those men had a bull's-eye on their back," the voice said.

I could not add one plus one. My mind had been stunned. I was dazed, not unlike being in shock, and my body didn't fare much better. "You and your husband will reunite. I am making it brand-new," the voice boomed. Then a map of California was before me and a big red star and the state's northern tip.

I knew in that instant I needed to go there wherever that was. The house was now quiet, and it was beginning to look like home again. Did my neighbors hear this commotion? What would I tell them? I somehow got to my feet and looked out the patio doors to the intense late afternoon sun. A giant colorful bird like a toucan flew from the top of my 1,600-square-foot ranch, and it had a fifty-foot wingspan. How did it fit on my roof? As that gigantic bird flew from my roof into the distance in front of my eyes, I saw it was carrying a little bird on its left wing. The little bird held tight as the gigantic wing did what wings on birds do when in flight, and I heard, "Fear not. I am carrying you."

> And you shall seek me, and find me when ye shall
> search for me with all your heart. (Jeremiah 29:13)

I did book a flight to Redding, California, to Bill Johnson's Bethel Church. I had been to a conference a year prior at which

Bill and his wife were ministering. I recognized his obedience to the Holy Spirit as he ministered to the churchgoers. My funds were tight; and as always, if my meager finances can get me what I need, then I take that as a confirming sign if it all works, and this trip was no exception.

I was going for two days. The area of Redding is easy to navigate. The weather had cooled down from the 111 degrees just a few weeks prior. The second night was the healing service and the reason I attended. Pastor Johnson calls out in what seems to be a random fashion of people who need healing when he hears the Spirit. I had high hopes.

Pastor Johnson called the second group to the altar. I was standing to the right of a tall blond man who had a cloudy right eye. The ministers approached him and asked if he believed the power of God sufficient to heal him. He said, "Yes."

As I looked over at the man in the right eye socket, I saw a swirling cyclone. It tossed my stomach slightly, looking at it, and then it stopped; and a brilliant blue eye filled the socket. As I peered at the man's left eye, I could see a color variance. As the thought fixed itself to my brain, the right eye took on the color of the left eye. I was next, and down I went. I remember waking up, and several people were looking over me, saying they had been praying as I lay there. I thanked them and got off the floor and returned to my seat. I felt no heat, no zips of electricity. Nothing indicating the cancer was expunged, but I had faith.

My flight home was later that evening, and I said goodbye to a few people I had met, and I walked toward the parking lot. There is a prayer house on a stream at the far side of the parking lot. I chose to walk through as I made my way to my car. There are two doors on either end with a vestibule for each. As I walked through the prayer house, I saw a man walking toward me. I knew this man but from where? As a nurse, one can encounter hundreds of people we have met. I just learned to accept that is the case and leave it at that.

As the man got closer, he looked at me, and he said, "What are you doing here?"

It was the minister from Vietnam. He went on to tell me he felt terrible about giving me that word at the church back east.

"Don't be silly. That word saved me. Thank you for your obedience to utter it," I said.

Seeing that prophet was my sign. The sign I needed to say I was healed, which indeed I was.

I am by this time well versed in the ways of God. While I don't have a local church, I tithe to other places of worship where I receive good teaching. I think of myself as a fully vested member of the body of Christ in a global sense.

I understand the spiritual realm of God. We battle not against flesh and blood but with the rulers of and the authorities of powers of darkness.

I had to repent for using a Ouija board game as a child and horoscopes and tarot. God told me heaven and earth is like an Oreo cookie. On earth as it is in heaven is the two-chocolate cookies. The white filling is the second heaven described in Daniel 10:12–13,

> Then he said to me, "Fear not, Daniel, for from the first day that you set your heart to understand and humbled yourself before your God, your words have been heard, and I have come because of your words. The prince of the kingdom of Persia withstood me twenty-one days, but Michael, one of the chief princes, came to help me, for I was left there with the kings of Persia."

The prince of Persia in this story was in the creamy layer of the cookie, the second heaven. The second heaven is where the divine and demonic realm can exist. I had the pleasure of talking to a few people who had a near-death experience, and the men are to go through the second heaven to get to heaven proper. The man is carried arm in arm with God's angels on either side. Bright light beams help to see the surrounding sights. The men I have talked to say they were never so terrified. One said he was in Vietnam, and he thought he has had seen everything as ghastly horrible as possible, but his chaperoned trip was far worse. It seems women are spared this horrid educational side trip was provided a solo ride up a white tube if the need to go to heaven arises.

As you can imagine, people are reluctant to discuss things of the Spirit that surpass what seems normal. My question is, Who decides what is normal?

Starbucks

I had just come back from a conference with Bobby Conner and a few other evangelists. It was always a powerful time, and God moved mightily in each service. God's angels were in abundance. I know I love coffee. Love it. I was concerned the love was out of control. Nothing can compete with the sweetness of my Lord. I had a daily Starbucks habit. Maybe I should stop drinking coffee. I put the exact change in my jeans pocket for the cost of a grande cup with one shot of flavoring. I like mint in my coffee.

I walked to the counter, and the barista said to me, "How would you like to try our new mint flavor in today's coffee?"

"Sure," I said. I reached into my pocket.

The barista said, "Oh, no, this is on the house today."

"Oh, thanks."

Truth be told that new mint was too dense or something. I will stick with the original mint.

I went back the following day, and one of the original baristas from the day before was there.

"How did you like that new mint flavor?" he asked.

"I didn't. I will stick with the original mint, please," I said.

"Okay, no problem," he said.

I had the original exact change still in the jeans' pocket from the day before. I reached my hand in my pocket to get the money.

"Oh, no. You are participating in an experimental run. On the house today," he said.

I was beaming. This was blowing my mind.

"I am glad I could make you happy," he said.

"That you did. Thank you," I said.

It went like this for the rest of the week with one or another of the baristas giving me a free cup of coffee for five straight days.

Okay, God, thank you!

> So, whether you eat or drink, or whatever you do, do
> all to the glory of God. (1 Corinthians 10:31)

The fruits of the spirit include the following:

Love, patience, and faithfulness

Joy, kindness, and gentleness

Peace, goodness, and self-control

Do you recognize the fruits of the spirit in yourself? I had to work on patience. Then God gave me a job that honed that skill magnificently. If I do say so, I gave God charge over my work life.

I had a prophetic word, and then a prophet looked at me and chuckled.

"No, you have not worked too many places, and you have always gone where God had sent you."

That was a sweet word.

Almost all that we know about the Spirit of God, we understand through the teaching of Jesus. Most of the scriptures about the Spirit of God are in the New Testament. Genesis of course in the first chapter, second verse reminds us:

> The earth was without form and void, and darkness
> was over the face of the deep. And the Spirit of God
> was hovering over the face of the waters.

Isaiah the prophet makes mention of the Spirit of God in Zachariah 4:6,

> Then he said to me, "This is the word of the LORD
> to Zerubbabel: Not by might, nor by power, but
> by my Spirit, says the LORD of hosts."

CHAPTER 9

Next Steps

J. C. Penney's Shoe Department

I WAS SUDDENLY thrust into a state of lack as my job closed down. No warning, just closed. I was being pulled from all angles financially.

I had an envelope budgeting system. It worked. I need new shoes for work. I had an interview the following week, an office job for a nurse. I needed clogs and business clothes. I went to the sales clerk's desk as I saw no clogs on display. "Seasonal item", I was told. The clerk asked my size. She disappeared into the storeroom. The girl appeared with two shoeboxes in hand. I had already decided black shoes would be best. "We have two pairs in your size. Navy and brown."

"No black?"

"No black, but if you buy one pair, you will get the second pair free of charge. Do you want to pay for the navy shoes?"

"Yes. Thank you. I love navy shoes."

Be not ye therefore like unto them: for your Father knoweth what things ye have need of, before ye ask him. (Matthew 6:8)

My job interview on the psych ward

I was interviewing at my old hospital; HR had called me. I didn't know I had applied to the locked psych unit. This unit was miles removed from the main hospital area. I doubt few of the PACU nurses even knew of its existence. The walls were all white. It was clean but old. The three people who interviewed me looked puzzled. Finally, the lead interviewer said, "Why did HR send you?"

"They probably sent me because I am really good at taking care of people," I said.

All three of the people chuckled. Honest to God, it was the weirdest interview I had ever been on. I went to the cafeteria to get a cup of coffee. I saw a unit secretary I knew. "What are you doing here today?" Linda asked.

I told her.

"Well, if you get the job, we will never know," she said.

"That would be something," I said, laughing.

"Yeah, good luck with the job. I am certain you got it."

I put the lid on the coffee and walked to my car. It would have to be God if I get this job. A job I don't think I wanted nor am I qualified for.

> My grace is sufficient for thee: for my strength is
> made perfect in weakness. (2 Corinthians 12:9)

I got the job on psych, and I was finished with the extended orientation, and it would be spring in about six weeks. I love spring. There are usually sections in a psyche ward as there are a variety of patients with mental difficulties, and some can be volatile. I had such a heart for my patients. Once they knew I understood about Satan, they opened up considerably. Satan somehow provided a life review and a suggestion of ending the life. The decision that life is no longer worth living is a choice with lots of pressure.

The people I knew who checked out and checked back while in the hospital never mentioned a life review. A life review happens when a permanent pass for heaven is in hand. Once that happens,

Jesus reviews the person's life with them. Where does this info for the review from? Heaven has a library, and the Bible says a book of life holds all believers' names. I have never heard about a file drawer of info in heaven, just a book.

I understood my patients that had attempted to take their own lives needed to repent to God for their actions. So many of my psych patients had read the Bible and had a decent biblical understanding. The nurse who followed my schedule on evenings cornered me one day at 3:10 p.m.

"What are you doing?" he asked.

"What do you mean? I am trying to go home."

"Room 1906, 1911, and 1920 are all on their knees at the side of their beds, praying," he said.

"I know. They are repenting to God for their actions," I said.

"Wow," he said.

My Dream in a White Pickup Truck

I was picked up by a red-headed man in a white pickup truck. I felt it might be David of the Bible. He drives me far away from home. He was a talker. I needed to see this place he said. We finally arrived at a big house in a cute village type of place. We walked in the front door. I met the family that lived there; they were very sweet. The butcher, the baker, and the candlestick maker is what I wrote in my journal.

I have amassed a large number of written journals. Every year, I list and thank God for all of the provisions provided in the previous year. Because God was now in control of my work life, some of that provision was unemployment pay.

You will not usually know when God is pulling strings for you. You may have a vague idea but nothing strong enough to call it a clue. I had made many friends in my nursing profession; I felt I had matured as a believer in incredible ways. I believed God could count on me to partner with Him in any way possible. Do not think for one minute my life was perfect, hardly. Working in chaos was the norm on unemployment or not.

Ten years went by, and I no longer worked in psych. I had a strong sense that I would be moving and even where to, but it made no sense. I told my neighbor I thought I would be moving. He asked when, and I told him. He seemed as puzzled as I did.

God had gotten me a job at JCPenney's in the drapery department and a job as a real estate agent (again). A friend's husband was ill, and I was helping them weekly, and that was sixty miles one way from home. I listed my tiny ranch home with no clear place to land. That was not my style. I was no longer a big risk-taker.

One day driving to my friends, I saw the house. My ex-husband loved brick houses. Maybe he was right; brick houses are a good investment. God moved mighty, and I had the funds with the sale to buy the house. It required much work and a few teams of capable men over three years to make it a home: the butcher, the baker, and the candlestick maker.

Then one day, it hit me; this was my dream in the white pickup truck. I was a princess in a palace, and God made it happen. The family that I knew belonged to this house visited me in this place that was somehow ours. What a blessing that was for all of us!

My Vision of Heaven

I was caught up in a vision, the first one ever. I was up in heaven in the marriage hall. It was a massive place with a ninety-foot ceiling. At first sight, I thought there was wallpaper on the wall. Wallpaper in heaven? Then I was taken a little closer to the wall, and it appeared there were postage stamps on the wall. I was taken a little closer, and I could see they were black wooden frames with glass covering optic white paper that had calligraphy writing. I was looking at Kathrine Stylops married to Felix Menninger, Saturday, June 24, 1949, plaque on the wall.

My gaze was directed to the right where there was an amber glow emanating from the gallery at the end of the hall, and I heard those are the champions who stuck together through all storms, clung to love keeping their vows, and I honor them.

What was I was stepping on? Oh, the floor was covered with broken wood and glass and crumpled paper. Why hadn't anyone swept the floor? How sad could God be that we have trashed marriage with Satan's help. I felt the intensely littered floor was a statement. See what you've done? Then I looked and saw optic white papers in glass that looked like a horse kicked it or a shot hit it. Some frames had one wooden edge; some frames were empty. My heart was breaking. What about all these families torn apart never to be the same? I panicked slightly. Where is my and my beloved's optic white certificate? I looked in the corner six rows up. There it was— no frame, no wood, the optic white paper was hanging on a nail. My heart sank. Our optic white paper did not belong on the floor to be trampled on. We had a good marriage, not perfect but darn good. I asked if it ever got windy in the wedding hall? I received no answer, and it started to rain.

Be devoted to one another in love. Honor one
another above yourselves. (Romans 12:10)

Who Is That Knocking on My Door?

I had an excellent friend. We had been friends for seventeen years. I had trained her for a job she was taking. We had been through thick and thin together. We were way different and just so much alike. I could never figure that out. I had saved Christmas once after she burnt the roast and everything else in the oven on Christmas morning, her company still four hours away. Her husband helped me in numerous ways, always helping me save lots of money on building supplies and other such things. He even told me not to pay anyone to take down a substantial twisted willow I had in the backyard. That lovely monstrosity was all mine. That tree he said was worth a small bundle.

Who is that standing knocking at my kitchen door? It took me a few moments to recognize the person.

I opened the door. We had not talked in I don't know how long; she had written me off more than once, and I was in a word done.

She is hugging me, telling me in one hundred-per-mile manner of speech that she had a revelation of God and Satan. She says I am the one who was the model. And on it went. I was suspicious. I mean, suspect. I gave her coffee, and we sat down for a few minutes, and she left hugging me again and saying God bless me. I nearly fell over.

She has been gone an hour, and I know if this is real, a genuine conversion, that she would have forgiven her siblings, all of whom I knew. That would be the litmus test. Well, as it turns out, they have all been talking and texting, and the one said it's weird but good.

I was still in a bit of shock when I go to bed. I woke in the morning and immediately remembered I took her to a prophet years prior, and she was told God was calling her to South America. I finally had peace. Yes, this must be real.

Then God said this is a type and shadow; a practice run if you will. Words cannot express my thanks for the dry run practice. I need to practice recognizing or believing God's legit move in the people I know and love.

> Delight thyself also in the Lord, and he shall give
> thee the desires of thy heart. (Psalm 37:4)

Speaking in tongues

Speaking in tongues is a spiritual language. All believers should desire to speak in tongues. Spiritual language is the language of heaven. I pray often and sometimes for lack of drive or ambition or knowing what to pray for. I find praying in tongues is a valuable tool to communicate with God. Once you are baptized in water, the spiritual language is usually born. Some can discern the spoken words as offered in speaking tongues.

When I speak, I hear my language from Asian sounding to a Czech Republic stiff tongue.

I was out of ministry service, and it was one night. It was late, and I stopped at the only gas station open to get gas.

There were cars circled around the store. I was sitting in my car out at the roadside, waiting for a pump spot to open. It was June, and the night air was warm. I saw a tall girl with a mop of auburn hair on top of her head pumping gas at the outer pump and talking in a singsong way her spiritual language. I could not discern what type of language it sounded like as I was too far away. She was lost in her endeavor as she pumped gas.

Then I noticed at the pump closet to the building a tall dark-complected man fell to his knees at his car door side. His hands clasped together as if in prayer.

As the tall girl wailed her spiritual language, the man on his knees began asking for forgiveness to God in a loud voice. All I could hear was, "God, God, God, help me."

Someone came up to my open car window and asked if I saw what was going on. We decided she was speaking a Middle Eastern language in her spiritual language, or that the new convert could discern spiritual language.

The powers of darkness are real. Satan knows Jesus is coming, and he wants to inhibit that with everything he has. The saving grace is that Christ is greater. The darkness cannot consume the light. The anointing of the Holy Spirit is sufficient in its power to overcome the darkness. Do you think the US NSA is snooping on us is terrible? Satan lays in wait, baiting the trap whenever he sees an opportunity. Satan is the father of all lies and the master of the bait and switch.

Have you ever fallen prey to a bait and switch when buying tires, entering into contracts, and other such endeavors? I had been working for companies outside of the United States, and one day, God said, "Are you done being bait and switched?" These are not American companies, with the underpinnings on which America was built. That statement has been made obsolete with the COVID lockdown and the woke social values that have taken over in the COVID era. Generally and what should return once the church takes its rightful place in society is that the godly values return by a crush of public opinion.

In Matthew 6:23,

But if your eye is evil, your whole body will be full of darkness. If, therefore, the light in you is darkness, how great is the darkness!

In John 1:3–5,

All things were made by Him and without Him, was
not anything made that was made In Him, was life and
the life was the light of men, And the light shines in the
darkness, and the darkness comprehends It not.

I wish you well on your journey, trusting you will find what you are looking for in your deeper walk with God.

____

____

____

____

All the scriptural references come from King James Version of the Holy Bible; Expositor's Study Bible by Jimmy Swaggart Ministries, PO Box 262550, Baton Rouge, Louisiana, 70826.

Thank you for listening to my story. I hope that one day you will write your own. Whether you have walked with God or you don't know God yet, my hope for this book is that it will give you confidence that you can draw closer no matter what you have or haven't done up to this point. God is waiting to hear from you. Today, you can repent for your sins and tell him you believe and are thankful for what Jesus has done for you because God the Father loves you. If you are a child of God, today you can repent for your sin, and God does not see your sin because of the cross. Jesus took care of that for you. In the garden, when Eve and Adam had sinned, in losing their anointing and the glory of God that clothed them, they now stood naked.

God called Adam and said, "Where are you, Adam?" God was inviting Adam to confess his sin. No questions asked. And Adam said, "But the woman you gave me…" And he repented not.

This had enormous consequences. God, in His love and mercy, made way for the righteous to be blameless. We know that there will be a catching away of all the believers, but only God knows the day and hour of that event. The fact of the matter is hell is looking for souls to snatch today and is working on overdrive, trying to accomplish its mission—its mission to rule the world. And prevent the manifestation of God in the latter days.

Man was given authority on the earth according to the Bible. Matthew 28:18, Jesus gave the Great Commission to go unto all the earth and teach all nations, baptizing them in the name of Father, Son, and Holy Ghost. Satanic hordes often inhabit the political realm, any realm where control of the masses occurs. Schools are another example. Satan cannot do so without the agreement of a man or woman. It all started with Adam and Eve. Satan has the power to seek, kill, and destroy. With trickery and lies, his cunning ways lead to destruction and death. Satan is not some bumbling idiot. He lacks light, which means there is no love in him, no truth, and no revelatory understanding. He wants you to worship him. He wants your will and your soul. It is the revelatory understanding with souls given to God in truth that will save us until we, the believers, experience the catching away. The moment that occurs, the pit of hell opens, and the beast, the Antichrist, will come through the political realm into the world stage. The book of Revelation 9:1–12 describes the event.

Isaiah 14:9 says, *"Hell beneath is stirred up to greet thee at thy coming."* This greeting is for the human who agrees with hell and there is no love in them. The person who believes is called righteous before the Lord in truth. One is magnificent in all ways, and the other is a cruel bloodbath. Now is no time for your soul to dangle in the wind when you could be reaching out to God. Those who have depression don't know it. The people around them may suspect it. The same is with demonic possession. Remember those boys I encountered at the art fair? I remember how badly I thought I had messed up that encounter and the relief I had when God revealed the truth to me. I want to impress upon you that you must learn to hear God and attend to the whispers of the Holy Spirit to lead you in all truth. He is overjoyed that in situations put in your path to help others, when you stand equipped. Being fully able to help others find the kingdom of God for themselves. A Bible tract won't do it, save the paper. Jesus provided the human touch with spiritual backing. As we are heirs in Christ, Jesus have given the same power. These occurrences will most likely never be a cordial event, yet God is putting his hope in *you* to recognize the moment and make a difference as you, the believer, offer a spirit of Christ himself in that moment. There is nothing that compares to knowing that God has seen you with your willingness to serve Him in all things.

How does one approach the slippery slope to hell? When your eyes are off Christ, you can step into almost anything—very little of any good. Remember, God told me the day the movie reel ran through my eyes, and God said, "Those men all had bullseyes on their backs." I have never heard of God using a bullseye technique to show His people how much He loves them. Let's talk about what can potentially certify you as bullseye worthy. Sexual sin is the number one tool of Satan. Pornography, Infidelity. Money is the second tool. Bob Jones was a man for Kentucky who was a great man of God. He died and went to heaven and stood in line to see Jesus. Bob said when he got up to the Lord, he was greeted and asked to look to the left. There, Bob saw a line of people as long as the eye could see. These people had golf clubs, shoes, wardrobes of clothes, boats, wads of money, fancy cars, diamonds, cruise liners, and more glued all over to themselves. He couldn't believe what people were putting <u>before</u> God in their lives. You can have all these things and so much more when God is first in your life. Jesus asked Bob if he would go back and prevent those people from going to hell. With that, Bob was revived after having had a heart attack.

First Thessalonians 1 and 2 are must-read—words of Paul as he speaks to the church of whom he loves. As the church, today, God is calling us to look beyond ourselves. Calling us to fear not as we speak out if there was ever a time in the US when the current leadership do not represent the people and turn their backs on mankind with disdain. We, the church, must rise like never before to support the light and those who are walking in the light on a national and global scale. We must pray with one voice for the will of God to be done in our nations. We must call for God's glory and thank Him for hearing our call.

I pray that above all things, the Lord would bless you and give you amplified discernment and that your eyes and ears would be wide open to experience the manifest glory of God. Amen.

RAISED IN A warm and loving family, Bonnie Nilsson had support to question life. *How will you know unless you try their expression for risk-taking?* Her father taught her how to box when she was eleven. At nineteen, she knocked out an adorable police wannabe. They were in the same criminal justice program. As his tall frame wilted toward the floor, the room gasped. God pulled her out of criminal justice and landed her in a nursing career, and it was no small wonder. After her health was challenged, she began looking for God. It was like God was playing hide-and-seek.

Several of her patients had NDE or near-death experiences. She began to know things she had no right to know. It is called a word of knowledge That freaked out the people closest to her. She was shocked at the people she met who felt disqualified from finding God. Someone else could tell them about God. She would not recommend that. She was a repentant sinner, a nonperfect human, yet God met her where she was. Most of the fighting she did was with herself, not with God or anyone else. Having been to Africa and the UK, learning no matter where people may live, they want to know that God does not only exist but that God is for them and cares about them. She has heard God laugh and felt his tears. The forces of evil in today's world are in overdrive. There has come a time for every human to say "I am with God or not." She wrote this book to encourage each person to find and know God for who He is.